NEGOTIATION DOMINATION

UNSTOPPABLE STRATEGIES FOR REAL ESTATE MASTERY

PAUL FINCK

Copyright © 2025 by Paul Finck

All rights reserved. No part of this publication may be reproduced, distributed, or transmitted in any form or by any means without prior written permission from the publisher.

Published by Centric Press LLC and in collaboration with / Cesar R. Espino - CRE Companies LLC

Negotiation Domination / Paul Finck - 1ST Ed.

ISBN: 979-8-9930237-0-0 (eBook)
ISBN: 979-8-9930237-1-7 (PaperBack)
ISBN: 979-8-9930237-2-4 (HardCover)

Dedication

The more things change, the more things stay the same. I have spent 40 years of my adult life striving to be the best husband, father, and businessperson I can be. Over the decades, the industry or business I was building changed. It seemed like being a great father adjusted based on the age of the children I was fathering (all my children are now young adults). The husband I built myself to be has outlived its usefulness as I am now a widower. As much as all has changed, the core and focus remains: To be the best I can be at carrying on the essence of my original goal: to be the best I can be at what I am dedicated to doing.

This book marks the beginning of a new era in my journey, with my soulmate watching over me instead of being right next to me. This book is dedicated to my amazing wife, Deborah Finck, who will always be by my side in spirit at every negotiation, providing me with the strength and wisdom to carry forward for both of us. May the strength of character she exuded in her life be a guiding light for us all to live life to its fullest every day! We are blessed to be here!

Thank you to all my children who have been leading examples of this in their lives. May you always negotiate out of life the best the world has to offer. To all my children, thank you for being so amazing. If it wasn't for your collective support, this book and all I do would be impossible.

Table of Contents

Acknowledgments i
Prelude iii
Introduction ix

CHAPTER ONE 1
    The Maverick Mindset

CHAPTER TWO 9
    Who's At The Table

CHAPTER THREE 21
    The Psychological Maneuvers

CHAPTER FOUR 35
    The Negotiation Dance

CHAPTER FIVE 43
    Always Question

CHAPTER SIX 53
    Leverage Strategies
        How to Tilt the Field

CHAPTER SEVEN 65
    Beyond the Table
        Where the Real Negotiation Lives

BONUS 71
    The Deal Maker's Playbook
        10 Maverick Hacks to Win

About the Author 75

Acknowledgments

No great victory is won alone. *Negotiation Domination* is the product of decades of deals, thousands of conversations, and the relentless pursuit of excellence — and there are many people I must thank for shaping this journey.

First, to my family — Amanda, Alexandra, Stephen, Katerina, David, and Daniel — you are my greatest negotiation wins in my life. Your love, patience, and belief in me have been the unshakable foundation beneath every risk I've taken and every bold move I've made.

To Deborah — my wife, soulmate, partner, my angel, and forever inspiration — your unwavering support and brilliance still guide my every decision. You taught me that the greatest negotiations aren't across a table, but in the way we show up for the people we love. Your legacy is woven into every word of this book.

To my Maverick Tribe — clients, colleagues, and friends who have dared to think differently — you've sharpened my skills with every challenge you brought to the table. You've trusted me with your businesses, your deals, and your futures, and I am honored to have fought alongside you.

To the mentors, partners, and dealmakers who have pushed me to think faster, aim higher, and dig deeper — your influence has been priceless. You know who you are, and you know the battles we've won together.

To every reader of this book — thank you for being bold enough to pick up a playbook designed to disrupt the status quo. May these strategies empower you to walk into any negotiation with confidence, clarity, and the certainty that you can, and will, dominate the outcome.

This is more than a book. It's a movement. And

you're now part of it.

Let's go dominate.

~ *Paul Finck, The Maverick Millionaire*

Prelude

The Maverick's Journey

Welcome to *Negotiation Domination: Unstoppable Strategies for Real Estate Mastery*. Before we dive into the strategies that will transform your negotiation skills, let me share with you a bit about my journey and how I've come to master the art of negotiation.

I am Paul Finck, known as the Maverick. My path to becoming a successful entrepreneur, speaker, and coach has been anything but conventional. With over 40 years of experience in sales, marketing, and entrepreneurial ventures, I have navigated the highs and lows of the business world, always seeking out innovative and effective ways to achieve success.

The Early Days

My journey began in the competitive world of sales. From my first job knocking on doors in the Medical Field in midtown Manhattan to selling high-ticket consultations, I quickly realized that the key to success wasn't just about having a great product or service—it was about how well I could negotiate. Early on, I learned that those who master negotiation could command higher prices, secure better deals, and build stronger relationships.

Building the Maverick Empire

As my career and life progressed, I ventured into real estate, personal development, and coaching. Each new venture presented unique challenges and opportunities, but the common thread was always negotiation. In real estate, I learned how to buy and sell properties at optimal prices. In personal development, I discovered how to negotiate partnerships and collaborations that expanded my reach and impact. As a coach, I honed my ability to teach others these critical skills, helping entrepreneurs and business leaders achieve their success.

The Maverick Mindset

One of the most significant turning points in my career was realizing the importance of our mindset in this equation. It wasn't enough to know negotiation techniques—I needed to embody an attitude of confidence, resilience, and creativity. I began to approach every negotiation with a maverick mindset, unafraid to think outside the box and challenge the status quo. This mindset has allowed me to turn seemingly impossible situations into opportunities for growth and success. And in turn, build a life of abundance.

Creating Win/Win/Win Scenarios

Throughout my career, I have always strived to create win/win/win scenarios. This means not just winning for myself, but also ensuring that my partners, clients, and stakeholders all benefit from the deal. This approach builds trust, fosters long-term relationships, and ultimately leads to greater success for everyone involved. The strategies you'll learn in this book are designed to help you achieve these win/win/win outcomes in your negotiations.

Teaching and Inspiring Others

Over the years, I have had the privilege of sharing my knowledge and experience with thousands of people through seminars, workshops, and one-on-one coaching. I've seen firsthand how mastering negotiation can transform lives and businesses. My mission is to empower as many people as possible to achieve their fullest potential, and I believe that mastering negotiation skillsets is a crucial step on that journey.

The Purpose of the Book

The purpose of this book is to provide you with a comprehensive guide to mastering negotiation. Whether you are a seasoned professional or a beginner, this book is structured to offer practical, actionable strategies that you can implement immediately. By understanding and applying these techniques, you will be able to navigate negotiations with confidence and achieve outcomes that benefit all parties involved.

In today's competitive world, the ability to negotiate effectively is more critical than ever. Deals are made or broken in moments, and those who come prepared with the right tools and mindset will always have the upper hand. This book aims to be your go-to resource for developing those tools and honing that mindset.

The ROI of Reading This Book

Investing your time in reading *"Negotiation Domination"* will yield significant returns in multiple areas of your life. **Here's what you can expect to gain:**

Financial Gain

By mastering these negotiation strategies, you will be able to secure better deals, command higher prices, and save money on purchases. Although the focus of our discussions here will be real estate, you can apply these same strategies to anything in your life to achieve better outcomes. Whether you're negotiating a business contract, a salary increase, or a major purchase, these techniques will help you maximize your financial outcomes. Imagine winning thousands more per deal simply by implementing the strategies outlined in this book.

Professional Advancement

Effective negotiation skills are highly valued in any professional setting. By demonstrating your ability to negotiate successfully, you will stand out as a valuable asset to your organization. This can lead to promotions, greater responsibilities, and more significant opportunities. As you become known for your negotiation prowess, your reputation as a skilled and strategic thinker will grow, opening doors to new career advancements.

Personal Empowerment

Negotiation is not limited to the boardroom. It is a critical skill in everyday life, from resolving conflicts to making decisions with family and friends. By learning these techniques, you will gain greater control over your interactions and outcomes. You will be able to influence situations to your advantage while maintaining positive relationships. This empowerment extends beyond material gains, fostering confidence and assertiveness in all areas of your life.

Enhanced Relationships

Successful negotiations create win/win/win scenarios that strengthen relationships. Whether in business or personal life, people appreciate fair and mutually beneficial outcomes. By mastering these strategies, you will build trust and rapport with others, leading to long-term, fruitful relationships. People will want to work with you, knowing that you strive for outcomes that benefit everyone involved.

Strategic Thinking

The strategies in this book will also enhance your overall strategic thinking skills. You will learn to approach problems creatively, think on your feet, and adapt to changing circumstances. These skills are invaluable in any context, helping you to navigate complex situations with ease and confidence.

Continuous Improvement

Negotiation is an art that evolves with practice. By continually applying and refining these techniques, you will develop a mindset of continuous improvement. This mindset will serve you well beyond negotiations, encouraging you to seek growth and excellence in all your endeavors.

Let's Begin the Journey

As you embark on this journey with me, I invite you to adopt the maverick mindset. Be open to new ideas, be willing to challenge yourself, and be prepared to think differently. Negotiation is an art, and like any art, it requires practice, patience, and a willingness to learn. These strategies are designed to empower you, making you unpredictable and effective at the negotiation table. Predictability is the Achilles' heel of negotiators; by diversifying your techniques, you ensure that you're always a step ahead. I'm excited to share these strategies with you and to see how they will transform your negotiations and life.

Thank you for choosing to invest in yourself and your future. The strategies in this book have been honed over decades of experience and success. Now, they are yours to implement and adapt. Get ready to unlock the power of negotiation and achieve remarkable results in your professional and personal life.

~ Paul Finck **The Maverick**

Introduction

Every conversation is a negotiation. Every engagement (verbal and non-verbal) is a negotiation. We negotiate everything and with everyone about everything in our world. From my earliest days in sales and business, I discovered that everything is negotiation. I built my career closing deals in industries ranging from real estate to coaching to finance, learning that true power comes from understanding people and mastering influence. These techniques have transformed my life—financially and personally—and given me the freedom to create success on my terms. Now, I want to share them with you, so you too can negotiate fearlessly and achieve domination in your real estate business.

What Is Negotiation?

Negotiation is not just a skill. It's a way of life—a moment-to-moment mastery of communication, psychology, and timing. In its purest form, negotiation is the process of moving others to action: convincing, influencing, and aligning interests so that both sides walk away feeling like they have won. Whether you realize it or not, every conversation, every email, and every contract is a negotiation. And in real estate, negotiation isn't just helpful—it's the entire game.

Why It's Important—And What It Can Do for You

If you want to dominate in real estate, negotiation is your unfair advantage. The right words at the right moment can save you tens of thousands or make you six figures. Negotiation determines how much you pay, how quickly you close, and how much equity and control you retain. It's how you get the inside track on deals, outmaneuver competition, and create win-win results that build your empire. Without strong negotiation, you leave money, power, and opportunity on the table.

Who Am I, and Why Should You Read This Book?

I'm Paul Finck, known around the world as The Maverick. For over 40 years, I've built businesses, negotiated real estate deals worth over $30 million, and closed over $50 million in coaching and consulting sales. I've spoken on stages across the globe, led hundreds of bootcamps, and coached thousands of investors, professionals, and high-level deal makers. It all started with negotiations. I built everything I have through the power of influence, relationships, and strategic communication.

Why I'm the One to Write This Book

Because I've lived it, I've negotiated under pressure, walked away from million-dollar deals, and come back to the table with even better terms. I have stared down difficult sellers, rescued broken contracts, and used simple shifts in language to unlock deals others thought were dead. This isn't theory. These are the exact strategies I use daily. In this book, I reveal all my Maverick negotiation techniques that have helped me and my clients build wealth, freedom, and certainty in an unpredictable world.

If you're ready to take control of your real estate business and your life, this book is for you. The

Maverick path isn't always easy. But it's always worth it. Let's begin.

What's Next: Your Maverick Playbook Unleashed

Now that you understand the raw power of negotiation and why it's the single most profitable skill you can master, it's time to go deeper. Much deeper.

This isn't just another book of random tactics. *Negotiation Domination* is structured like a war manual and designed to build layer upon layer of influence, persuasion, and strategic firepower.

Over the coming chapters, you'll discover the full scope of what it takes to walk into any negotiation with confidence, control the energy in the room, and walk out with results most people only dream of.

We'll break this mastery down into **seven strategic sections**, each one tackling a different domain of the negotiation battlefield:

The Mental Chess Game: Regulate Your Emotions Before You Ruin the Deal

Before you ever open your mouth, the real battle starts between your ears.

You'll learn how to control your emotional state, how to read the other side's tells, and how to reframe fear, doubt, and hesitation into fuel. If you can't manage yourself, you'll never control the outcome.

Who's at the Table: Understand the Players and How to Engage Each One

Not every negotiation is one-on-one, and not every player wants the same thing. We'll decode how to identify key decision-makers, spot hidden influencers, and tailor your strategy to buyers, sellers, investors, partners, contractors, or even your team. Different players, different games. You'll learn how to win them all.

The Psychological Maneuvers: Advanced Influence Techniques During the Game

This is where the real Maverick tactics come alive.

You'll discover how to use body language, silence, pacing, mirroring, anchoring, and storytelling to move the negotiation in your favor. These are the invisible strings that pull the deal toward your outcome without force or friction.

The Dance: Maverick Moves That Shift Power in Your Favor

Negotiation isn't about bulldozing your way through—it's a dance.

We'll explore subtle yet powerful moves that allow you to stay in rhythm, take control of the tempo, and never appear desperate, aggressive, or out of sync. This is where elegance meets strategy and persuasion becomes irresistible.

Always Question: The Secret Weapon Most Negotiators Miss

The one who asks the questions owns the conversation.

You'll learn the exact questions to ask in every scenario, from opening the conversation to handling objections to sealing the deal. This section alone will transform your conversations, eliminate resistance, and keep you in control at every turn.

1. Leverage Strategies: How to Tilt the Field and Win Before You Even Sit Down

Real negotiation power isn't just in the conversation. It's in the preparation.

We'll unlock techniques to create leverage before the deal begins: controlling the frame, owning the agenda, managing urgency, and stacking authority in your favor. These strategies ensure you walk in already positioned to win.

2. **Beyond the Table: What Happens Before and After the Deal Matters Most**
Some of your greatest negotiation wins will happen outside the room.

We'll cover follow-up power plays, reputation-building, relationship dynamics, and how to turn one-time deals into lifetime allies. Plus, I'll show you how to audit and learn from every deal you do—so you get better, faster, with every interaction.

Your Mission Starts Now
Each section of this book builds on the last. This is a complete system—tested over decades, proven across industries, and is now ready to become your edge in every conversation.

You're not just going to read about negotiation. You're going to embody it.

Because domination isn't about being louder, tougher, or more aggressive, it's about being smarter, sharper, and more intentional.

So take a breath. Grab your pen.

Get ready to underline, highlight, and take notes like your business depends on it—because it does. The game is on.

Let's play to win.

CHAPTER ONE

The Maverick Mindset

To become a master negotiator in real estate, you must first develop a powerful mindset. A powerful mindset operates with focus and deliberate intent. A powerful mindset knows what the outcome is before it arrives.

You must know what is desired and exhibit behaviors congruent with that desire. Easier said than done? Of course.

However, it is the keystone to any successful negotiator and the foundation for utilizing all the strategies I am sharing with you here. The more effective you are in regulating your emotions, the more effective you will be at executing the negotiation techniques that drive high-dollar outcomes. The foundation of all negotiation is internal: it begins with you.

BELIEF IS YOUR FIRST BARGAINING CHIP
Before you can influence anyone else, you must first

convince yourself. You must believe. **Believe in yourself**. Believe in your business model. Believe that what you're doing is effective, ethical, and valuable. And most importantly, believe that the number you are offering—or counter-offering—is the best deal they will get, and they would be foolish not to take it.

Everything about you broadcasts that belief. Everything around you will carry your message forward! Your body language, the tone in your voice, the slight up or down pitch of your last word; all will give you away unless YOU BELIEVE. When you have such incredible confidence in who you are and what you do, THEY will have confidence in the offer you are negotiating. When you believe at a deep level that you are going to get a certain price and a certain result, your chances of actually getting it go up exponentially.

Next: **you MUST not care!** To be effective at creating the legacy money you are dreaming of, you must be willing to leave the table. If you must win every hand, you will never win the whole game. Your ability to negotiate effectively is in direct proportion to your ability to walk away. Early on in my career, I remember negotiating a deal, and it was $30K spread between our current offer and my target number. Because I knew it was still a good deal for the other side for $30K less and because I knew the owner wanted to and needed to sell, I "put all my chips on the table" in an all-or-nothing counteroffer. "I will pay x and not a dollar more. Take it or leave it," I then told them to call me after they had thought it over. Truth be told, after I hung up the phone, my wife and I just sat there holding hands, held our breath, and prayed. Thirty minutes later, I got the call, "Yes! Offer is accepted!" You have got to be willing to lose big to have a chance at winning big.

It begins with understanding that your greatest power often lies in your willingness to walk away. I once negotiated a 20% discount on a multi-family property simply because I wasn't afraid to leave the table when the terms weren't right. Twice, I stepped back, only for the seller to pursue me with better offers. This is the essence of **Walk Away Power**—a firm belief that no deal is worth sacrificing your standards or your future profits. In poker, the ability to know when to hold and when to fold is infamous. When you say, "I'm not sure this deal works for me as-is. I'm going to step back for now and pursue other opportunities," you're signaling strength and confidence that often compels the other side to reconsider. Sometimes the best negotiation technique is to say "Next" and be willing to do so. Sometimes it is NOT the deal you should be in. And often, the attitude of being willing to walk away will have the other party giving you all you want to get you to stay. The side that is less vested in the outcome WILL be the stronger force in the negotiations.

Confidence in Uncertainty

Alongside this is the crucial skill of maintaining **Confidence in Uncertainty**. The world of real estate is filled with incomplete information and shifting circumstances. My experience in competitive markets taught me that waiting for perfect clarity means missing opportunities. Instead, I make offers contingent upon due diligence, saying, "Let's put it under contract and I'll verify details along the way (during inspection). If it doesn't fit, we'll pivot." This approach allows movement without fear, a vital quality when time-sensitive deals arise.

Equally important is Emotional Control, or, to be more accurate, **Emotional Regulation**. In negotiations, emotions run high—sellers might provoke you, try to unsettle you, or pressure you into revealing more than you should. For example, once, a seller insulted my offer, attempting to goad me into admitting his maximum price. I remained composed, repeating his original terms, and ultimately secured the deal on his conditions. Calm statements like, "I understand you feel strongly about your price. Let's focus on how we can structure this to work for both of us. Remember to keep the discussion productive and remove the emotional sting from heated exchanges.

Success also demands preparation (mental preparation), and that's where **The Maverick Mental Rehearsal** comes in. Before any significant negotiation, I recommend a ritual of mental preparation. Visualize the discussion in your mind, anticipating objections, and practicing your responses. For example, before negotiating a $1.5 million commercial building, I mentally rehearsed every possible pushback and how I would answer every concern without losing composure. When objections arise, imagine your response and how you would handle each of them easily and readily. When all happened in the real world, and these same objections would come up, they all got taken care of as if I was reading from a script since I had already faced them in my mind a dozen times.

Finally, every great negotiator must establish a **Winning Identity**. You need to present yourself as a serious, professional investor who is both credible and decisive. Do this by maintaining a professional appearance, speaking with authority, and referencing past successful deals. When I say, "My team and I have closed dozens of similar deals. I'm looking to move quickly and professionally here as well." I am planting seeds of confidence in the minds of sellers and partners alike.

All these strategies work powerfully on their own, but their true strength lies in how they combine. When I approached the seller of a distressed 12-unit building, the conversation was tense. The seller was aggressive and emotional. I used Emotional Control to stay calm, projected Confidence in Uncertainty by making an offer even without complete rent rolls, and displayed Walk Away Power when the seller pushed back too hard. My earlier Mental Rehearsal prepared me for each objection, and my Winning Identity as a credible investor gave me authority. Two days later, the seller returned, accepting my original terms. This victory resulted in a $180,000 reduction in the asking price.

Maverick Mindset

This is the **Maverick Mindset** in action. It's not about gimmicks or tricks or universal mystical ya-ya; it's about showing up as the most prepared, confident, and professional version of yourself. When you internalize these principles, you'll approach every negotiation with clarity and strength. As you move forward in this book, remember: you are the expert. Remain calm, confident, and ready to walk away when needed. That's the first step toward Negotiation Domination.

Interested in maintaining or achieving the maverick persona, click here
https://www.NegotiationDomination.com/Manifesto

Bonus Negotiation Strategies

Lead with emotions! When you have the Maverick Mindset in place, everything else becomes easier because emotion is the driving force behind all behavior. Once you can regulate your own emotions, you can use them effectively in your communication patterns. We decide emotionally and justify with logic. In all sales and especially in negotiations, the most effective methodology is to focus on the emotional reasons to move the other side. Once they have decided, give them all the logical reasons you can to justify the decision they have already made. It is the emotion that moves and influences them; the logic simply gives them ways to justify the purchase.

One example of this and one of the most underestimated yet highly effective negotiation strategies is **The Praise Proposition.** At its core, this tactic revolves around identifying and acknowledging the ego needs of the players involved, especially when dealing with individuals who crave recognition and affirmation. These are the people who light up when their intelligence, experience, leadership, or uniqueness is validated. When you feed that need for emotional significance with genuine, targeted praise, you unlock an almost irrational level of rapport and trust. This high-ROI move is so powerful because it costs you nothing but attention and intention—yet it can yield everything from faster agreements to more favorable terms.

Learn how to identify IN SECONDS the priorities of others. Click here
https://www.NegotiationDomination.com/personalities

When done effectively, you are not fabricating flattery; you're highlighting authentic strengths that align with your goals. When delivered sincerely and strategically, praise becomes a gateway to influence. These individuals will often lean toward your proposal simply because you made them feel like the smartest person in the room. In their eyes, you "get them," and people say yes to those who validate their worth. Use this tool wisely, consistently, and with integrity, and you'll find it gives you a powerful edge in negotiations that few ever learn to wield.

As can often be the case, emotions can go both ways. When you are in control and can regulate effectively, emotions can be brought to the surface at whim. Take, for example, **The Fire-starter Play.** When diplomacy is too comfortable and the deal is dragging—or worse, drifting—ignite *The Fire-starter Play*. This is where you create intentional conflict: a flash of heat, a jab of emotional intensity, a disagreement too sharp to ignore. It throws off their rhythm, disorients the expected flow, and pulls everyone into fight-or-flight. Now you control the flame.

Used strategically, the fire can serve two purposes: first, as a **distraction**, forcing a reset while you gain psychological ground; second, as a **behavior correction**, sending a clear signal that crossing certain lines will *burn*. Once scorched, they'll avoid the flame at all costs. They'll sidestep confrontation, bend over backward to stay on your good side, and overcompensate in your favor—all to avoid another flare-up. It's not about chaos—it's about power projection. Light the fire once, and they'll spend the rest of the negotiation making sure you never strike that match again.

Power Plays

Let's add a few power plays to the mix:

Speak Last. In every negotiation, resist the urge to be first. Let the other side speak their price, terms, or limits first. When they lay down their cards, you gain critical knowledge. Often, they will reveal more than they intend. All great information you can use to your advantage in the process. If you speak first, you limit your potential upside. You may even end up negotiating against yourself. When you listen first, you learn.

Present All in Writing. Written is better than verbal. The moment you write it down, your offer gains gravity. Written terms feel final and real—they're more likely to be taken seriously and less likely to be debated. People accept what's in writing with more readiness, even reverence. It frames you as the authority and the offer as legitimate.

Paint Pictures. People make decisions emotionally and justify them logically. Instead of just presenting numbers or terms, create a vision. Help them see what it feels like to be on the other side of the deal—stress-free, wealthy, empowered, relieved, or respected. When they see it in their mind, they buy into it.

Power Pause. When they ask for something big, pause, and let the silence hang in the air. When you pause deliberately, it creates uncertainty. It forces them to question their request. The longer they sit in silence, the more they question their position. Let them sweat.

Dumb It Down. Don't play the genius. People let their guard down with those who feel relatable, even slightly naive. Use this strategically. Ask simple questions. Be a student. When they underestimate you, they make mistakes. You win quietly.

THE MAVERICK MINDSET STACK

When you combine these elements—unshakable belief, emotional regulation, strategic silence, written authority, empathetic visioning, and a willingness to walk away—you create the Maverick Mindset. It is the bedrock of everything that follows because until you learn to control yourself, you will never control the room. Every conversation is a negotiation. Every moment is a message. Believe deeply. Present in writing. Ask again. Paint the outcome. Speak last. Stay calm. Pause powerfully. Listen louder than you speak. Be willing to lose the deal to win the game.

CHAPTER TWO

Who's At The Table

In real estate, negotiation is not just about properties—it's about people. Every deal involves stakeholders with unique interests, pressures, and hidden motivations. As a Maverick, I've learned how to read the players at the table and tailor every conversation accordingly.

For example, when one of my clients was buying a commercial property—a 14,000 sqft building listed for $1.8 million—the seller seemed polite but firm on price, rejecting all offers below asking. Instead of arguing, we decided to study the players involved. By quietly speaking with the broker's assistant and asking the right questions, we learned the broker stood to lose a significant bonus if the deal closed below a certain number. We approached the broker privately and proposed a commission structure that protected the broker's earnings while allowing the seller to accept a $1.65 million price. The broker agreed and convinced the seller to lower the price. Without understanding the broker's true interest, my client might have lost the deal entirely. (We will discuss the questions to ask later.)

The reason this deal could have gone terribly wrong had everything to do with recognizing who was at the table. In this case, it wasn't about the buyer or the seller and their individual needs or desires. It was about the agent's needs. You never know who you need to serve, and every deal is different. Be open to realizing who is an influencer in the deal and making sure they are happy.

Another time, during a four-family residential sale, I noticed tension between the seller's two adult children. Through strategic observation and gentle questioning, I discovered the children disagreed on selling timelines. One wanted a quick sale to cash out; the other feared losing rental income too soon. I proposed a delayed closing with partial funds released immediately, satisfying both siblings and securing the deal. You never know. (We will discuss asking more questions later and how to get information like this.)

These deals taught me that negotiation rarely hinges on numbers alone—it hinges on people. Understanding the players—their roles, fears, and incentives—is often the true secret to negotiating like a Maverick. That's why I always ask questions like, "Help me understand everyone's priorities so we can find the best way forward." I read subtle signals, ask strategic questions, and notice hidden agendas others miss.

I've learned that your real power in negotiation often comes not from the figures on paper but from what you know about the people sitting across the table. When you know their story, you hold the keys to unlocking the deal.

Let's get into a few strategic details centered around understanding who is at the table. The decision makers can be the sellers or the buyers in the equation, depending on your situation. I call them the **King and Queen**. You must make sure, in all negotiation situations, you are dealing with ALL the decision makers. Not just the ones that show up; ALL of them. Realize that when partners or husband/wife teams meet separately, they will use that to their advantage. "I have to check with my...." In that way, they have an out (a reason not to have an answer yet). When you ONLY meet with them together as a unit, you steal that ace tactic from them to use.

Most of the time, you have the more business-oriented or more outgoing member of a team or couple who is engaged in communication with you. This is where you must be diligent in getting all parties to the table. Always ask, "Besides yourself, who else will be involved in making the final decision other than you?" Some other ways to get to the same place: "Just so I understand the full process — who else do we need to get buy-in from before moving forward?" "If everything we discuss makes sense today, is there anyone else who would need to be involved before we move ahead?" "Who signs off on the final agreement or budget for this?" Any of these phrases will get you to the same result.

Once they say a person (or persons) is also part of their decision-making process, YOU MUST make sure you are sitting with all of them together. It is only then that you have a chance of closing them. It is only then that everyone is together to come up with a joint decision. Without this step, the excuses will pile up and leave you with lots of time and energy spent with zero chance of a sale. Consider yourself warned.

You may also have real estate agents in the real estate transaction. Usually, there would be a "listing agent" who represents the seller and sometimes even a "buyer's agent" who represents the buyer. It is common for a buyer to let the listing agent represent both sides of the transaction; however, it is NOT recommended. Instead, I love to bring in my own buyer's agent. I prefer to use the same buyer's agent for all my transactions because then he already knows how I think and can anticipate my moves. With a buyer's agent on your team, you are now easily able to position them as an Arbitrator or intermediary, which can be a huge advantage. For instance, I position a "buyer's agent" between me and a seller to play "Good Cop/Bad Cop," where I can play the "Bad Cop" from afar (or the "Good Cop" when appropriate.)

Good Cop/Bad Cop (or Hope Giver/Hope Taker or Your Side/Their Side) is a two-person technique, with one person on the team taking the position of being hard, strong, absolute, and often extreme in their viewpoint, while the other team member engages as more giving, caring, and flexible. It can also work when you represent or are controlled by an entity or organization that is not directly involved in the negotiations, and yet, YOU have to answer to them. My company, my company policy, my boss, my accountant, my attorney, my spouse, my silent partner, my other clients who are not getting that good a deal, etc. They all can be the "Bad Cop." Positioning each team member effectively during the negotiations can create a huge advantage for the team as a whole.

Once you have the team members in place to use them, you have some additional negotiation strategies available. One of my favorites is what I like to call **"Send in the Subs."** In a team sporting event, whenever the momentum for the opposing side is overwhelming in their favor, the coach will call a timeout, or a time out with new players (subs). You can do that in our real estate negotiations as well. When you are not making headway in a negotiation, bring in new players or substitute some of the key players at the table. Just like in a sporting match, new players will change up the dynamics and give you a slight edge right away. New players will create new energy that often will change the momentum and the flow of the negotiations back into your favor.

For those times when you don't have team members to lean on and yet you still feel like the momentum is working against you, there is still hope. Simply create a **Break: a purposeful pause in the negotiations.** You can express this openly and honestly, or you can come up with another excuse. Either way, find a reason to step away from the negotiation table, figuratively speaking. Pause negotiations! The "break" will change the dynamics and flow of the negotiations.

One last powerhouse negotiation tactic for this category: **The Higher Authority.** When you are in a tight spot, when you cannot or simply don't want to answer a question just yet, when you want to maintain flexibility, control the tempo, or shift pressure without looking like the bad guy, call in the invisible partner. This invisible partner could be referred to as your spouse, your investor partner, or even a member of your board. Unfortunately, "they" have the final say, which is now beyond your control. You are simply the messenger and not the decision maker. You will transmit all info to this invisible power player and get back to them. This accomplishes two major keys: 1) It removes personal pressure on you, and 2) It creates additional space in the timeline to think and negotiate. You can float ideas, gauge reactions, and then "check with your higher authority" to pull back or push forward. It builds time and distance into the deal. And most importantly, it protects your position. If they push back too hard, you have plausible deniability: *"Hey, I love it too—but it's not up to me."* This gives you the upper hand while they're stuck negotiating with a ghost. Use the Higher Authority Close to deflect pressure, gain leverage, or sweeten your terms. It's the ace up your sleeve that says: *"I want to help you… but let me run it by my people."* In truth, *you are your people*—but they don't need to know that.

The other personalities

I've spent decades negotiating deals—multi-million-dollar real estate transactions, high-ticket coaching sales, partnerships in multiple industries—and through all of that, here's the truth that's held up every time:

You're never negotiating a number. You're negotiating with a personality.

That personality—how they think, how they react under pressure, what they value, and what they fear—*determines everything.* The speed of the deal. The objections you'll face. The way you have to close. If you miss it, you'll lose them. If you read it right, you can guide them anywhere you want them to go. Over the years, I've studied and tested dozens of personality frameworks—some complex, some elegant, some just plain confusing. But one system keeps delivering because it's **straightforward, adaptable, and built for the real world**. It's called **DiSC**, and it's the go-to tool in my Maverick toolbox when I'm training high-level real estate pros, sales teams, and entrepreneurs on how to win conversations without brute force.

Take your own assessment
https://www.NegotiationDomination.com/Assessment

It works because it's simple. Four main personality types. Each has predictable patterns. And once you understand those patterns, the whole game shifts.

The Four Types

Let's break it down in real-world terms, not academic fluff. These are the personalities sitting across the table from you right now—in the living room on a listing appointment, in the negotiation over a price drop, or at a kitchen table with an emotional seller trying to keep their life from falling apart.

The D – Dominant Driver

You know this one the second they walk in. Direct. Assertive. They talk fast, move faster, and **don't have time for the fluff**. They want results, control, and the fastest route from Point A to Point Closed. If you stall, they'll bulldoze you. If you talk too much, they'll lose respect. But if you come in with confidence, direct language, and a bottom-line solution, they'll respect the hell out of you. This is not where you lead with feelings. You lead with leverage. You move a D by saying, "Here's where we are. Here's what we can do. Which way do you want to win?"

The I – Influencer

They're the ones telling stories, laughing, and bonding. They want a connection. Energy. They buy based on *how the deal makes them feel* more than what the spreadsheet says. You try to drop a ten-page contract on them with itemized comps? You've lost them. But if you tell them a story about the last seller who used you and is now sipping margaritas in Costa Rica, they're leaning in. You close an I by building **rapport first, logic second**. Paint pictures. Use emotion. Let them feel excited before you ask them to sign. For an I, you must make it fun and exciting. Say something like, "Can you see yourself living here? Your bar can go here, dancing here, and the backyard can hold a ton of people! Let's toast to finding the perfect space!"

The S – Steady Supporter

These folks are calm, polite, and loyal to a fault. They don't like sudden change, and **they hate pressure**. They're the ones who nod through your entire presentation, ask very few questions, and then say, "We're just going to sleep on it." Not because they're stalling. They just need *time to feel safe*. You don't close an S by pushing. You close them by **building trust**. Step by step. Show you care. Repeat your points. Invite them forward. Don't drag them. You reassure them with" Let's take this at your pace. I'm here when you're ready, and I'll make sure every step is clear and easy." The followup, followup, followup. When they trust you, they'll sign and stick with you forever.

The C – Cautious Analyzer

This is the detail person. They want proof. They want systems. They want to know everything—from the property line measurements to the municipal water history. They *will wear you out* if you're not prepared. But when you are? They'll respect the fact that you came to the table with precision. You win with a C by giving them **everything they need to feel unburdened by human emotions and drama**. Present the comps, the inspection reports, and the ROI calculations. Tell them the exact numbers (no "kinda"). Say with a matter-of-fact tone, "I've run the comps across four similar properties within a quarter mile. Here's the breakdown. How long would you like to review the data? They will not be quick to sign, but once they see your logic holds up, they'll close *without regret*. And they'll defend you to everyone they know.

So, How Do You Use This?
To read people quickly, here are some quick reference points:
Are they fast-talking, results-driven? High D.

Are they bubbly, emotional, and connection-seeking? High I.
Are they steady, quiet, thoughtful? High S.

Are they analytical, slow-moving, data-focused? High C.

Once you spot their type, you **adapt your tone, your pacing, and your pitch** to meet them where they live. And once they feel understood, they trust you. And once they trust you, they follow you. That's the game. Selling isn't about saying the right thing—it's about saying the *right thing the right way to the right person.*

DiSC is your decoder ring. It gives you a blueprint to influence without pressure. It helps you move every deal forward with less friction and more flow. So before you walk into the next meeting, ask yourself, "Who am I saying it to?" DiSC. Once you know that, you will always know how to win. Grab your Maverick DiSC Playbook (specific techniques for each personality).

https://www.NegotiationDomination.com/MaverickDisc playbook

Let's shift gears for a moment and discuss the terrain you step into when you are working in the real estate space. In a perfect world, negotiations would be face-to-face, direct, and unfiltered. But in real estate? That's rarely the case. More often than not, you're dealing with a lawyer (or several) between you and the decision-maker. Real estate agents, attorneys, spouses, silent partners, even family members acting as "helpers"...

They all act as intermediaries, filters, or gatekeepers. And if you don't know how to work through them, your deal dies before it ever gets to the top.

First things first: you need clarity on who actually pulls the trigger. You must identify the true Decision-Maker. Is it the seller on the deed? Their spouse, who's quietly calling the shots? A business partner not even on the paperwork? Or the attorney who has veto power? Never assume that the person you're talking to is the only one you need to influence. Dig deeper. "Who else is involved in making this decision?", "Is there anyone else who'll need to review this before we move forward?", "How have decisions like this been made in the past?"

To uncover the power structure and move past gatekeepers, you must use subtle, non-threatening curiosity by planting seeds (which is an art form). You might not be able to influence the decision-maker directly. When that is the case, your best alternative is to shape what the intermediary says to them. HOW? Give them phrases they can repeat. Offer logical points that are easy to paraphrase. Use emotionally charged language they'll pass along even if they don't mean to.

Let's say you're negotiating with a seller's agent. You say: "We're offering $445K because the comps are all pointing in that direction, and we're the only offer willing to waive the inspection contingency. That gives your client speed and certainty. Not just money."

Armed with that information, the agent will talk to the seller. And instead of just saying, "They're offering $445K," they most likely will say, "They came in at $445K, but they're also waiving inspection. You'll have a clean close." The agent has now helped anchor your message without you even being in the room. Bring this to a pro level by deliberately giving the intermediary one emotional reason and one logical reason to pass along.

People remember logic. They *repeat* emotion.

Let's continue to make this even more fun. In many deals, the gatekeeper has someone *they* trust who's not in the negotiation. That might be a mentor, a business partner, or a more senior colleague. Your job? FIND OUT WHO THEY ARE and influence *that* person.

Again, you ask how? Ask questions that uncover who your intermediary respects. Look for ways to meet, speak with, or otherwise influence that trusted advisor. Imagine you're negotiating with an investor's assistant. She keeps saying, "Let me run this by the boss." Instead of just waiting, you do some digging. Turns out the "boss" listens to a local real estate attorney who helped him on a few big deals. You reach out to that attorney (or mention that you've worked with them before). You drop some praise about how smart that advisor is. Then, when your offer crosses the boss's desk, they're hearing it from someone whose opinion already matters. You're playing 3D chess while everyone else is playing checkers.

Unfortunately, the game often has players in it who are not your friends. Sometimes, for instance, the agent is more of a block than a bridge. They filter your message, insert their own agenda, and generally create friction instead of clarity. You will see this most often when agents don't believe in your offer, feel threatened by your knowledge or positioning, or have another buyer they favor (one of their peeps).

In this case, you don't attack. You must *out-position*. Be careful not to overstep by being overly respectful, ask a ton of clarifying questions, and offer to summarize your points in writing for "ease of communication." In this way, you will be able to transmit what you actually want to say, without the agents spinning on it.

How do you deal with Dual Agents? One of the murkiest waters in real estate is when the agent is representing both sides while clearly favoring one over the other.

You're now negotiating through someone who's not fully in your corner. So what do you do?

1. **Don't play victim.** - Assume they're biased and move accordingly.
2. **Use transparency as leverage.** - Say: "I know you're representing both sides, and I respect that. That's why I want to be ultra-clear in my communications so nothing gets lost or misinterpreted."
3. **Send everything in writing.** - This protects you and puts pressure on the agent to relay your position faithfully.
4. **Use the client as the final voice.** - Ask: "Would you be open to letting your client review this directly so they can make the best decision?"

You're not challenging the agent. You're appealing to fairness and accuracy. That puts the agent in a position where *not relaying* your offer feels negligent! Yeah - another win for the home team.

CHAPTER THREE

The Psychological Maneuvers

To win in real estate negotiations, you must understand what drives people, not just logically, but emotionally. Logic makes people think. Emotion makes them act. That's why mastering the psychological maneuvers is essential if you want to consistently close deals. (Doubly true when dealing with distressed properties or FSBO - For Sale By Owner - sellers since you have no one mitigating the emotions).

In many of these situations, you're not just negotiating price or terms; you're navigating pain, pride, and fear. Sellers may be emotionally attached to the home, grieving a loss, dealing with financial stress, or convinced that no investor truly has their best interest at heart. If you miss the emotional undercurrent, you'll miss the deal. Let me restate that: If you miss the emotion gym class, you will miss the opportunity!

I remember walking into an FSBO listing where the owner had lived in the house for 30 years. It wasn't just a property—it was his entire life story. Other investors had lowballed him, treated it like just another transaction, and walked away with nothing. I sat down with him at his kitchen table and said, "Tell me about what this house has meant to you." That question changed everything. He opened up about his late wife, his kids, and his retirement fears. And then he listened—really listened—when I explained how I could give him peace of mind, not just a check.

That's what persuasion looks like: not pressure, but empathy combined with authority. You listen with care, engage with their concerns, and then offer a solution that makes them feel seen and respected. I used a three-step approach:

1. **Acknowledge their story**: "I see how much love you've put into this place."
2. **Frame the offer as relief**: "Let me take the stress off your plate."
3. **Position yourself as their advocate**: "I'm here to create a win for you." (not to take advantage of your situation).

When you follow these steps, you reframe the negotiation from conflict to collaboration—just one example of how you can turn emotional resistance into trust.

Remember, high emotions equal low intelligence. When you can keep your cool while others around you are not, and you have clarity and confidence while others are being triggered emotionally, you win the day.

One seller I worked with was facing foreclosure and was overwhelmed. He couldn't think straight, so I broke the process into bite-sized wins. I said, "Let's take this one step at a time." I held his hand step by step as we walked through the steps. This approach got the contract signed in under 48 hours. When you master the psychology of persuasion, you become more than just a buyer or seller. You become the trusted expert they're looking for—the one who understands both the value of the property and the emotions attached to it.

Understanding the psychological journey a person goes on when selling a property is one of the keys to being able to play the "game" effectively. To reference this next technique, I am going to teach you a bit about science. Isaac Newton was a brilliant English mathematician, physicist, and astronomer who lived in the 17th century and is widely regarded as one of the most influential scientists in history. Among his many groundbreaking contributions, he formulated the three fundamental laws of motion that form the foundation of classical mechanics. These laws describe how objects move and interact with forces in the physical world. **Newton's First Law**, also known as the law of inertia, states that an object will remain at rest or move at a constant speed in a straight line unless acted upon by a force. **Newton's Second Law** explains how the force on an object is related to its mass and acceleration (**F = ma**). Finally, **Newton's Third Law** states that for every action, there is an equal and opposite reaction. Together, these laws revolutionized the way we understand motion and laid the groundwork for modern physics.

"Paul, what the heck does this have to do with negotiations?" Since we are beings made up of energy, these laws apply to us as well. Let's take one at a time. Newton's First Law, summarized, says an object in motion will stay in motion in the absence of any force acting against it. In Negotiations, the more you maintain the conversation and connection with your prospect, the more likely they are to complete the transaction with you. Every engagement with the other person leads to another engagement. Every text leads to another text. Every meeting leads to another meeting. Keep the connection alive.

Here is what is going on internally. The other person in this engagement (and it doesn't matter what side of the equation you are on), IF they start considering NOT doing business with you, is experiencing an uncomfortable imbalance between their actions and their thoughts. They are desperately unconsciously looking to justify the time they have spent with you. The ONLY way this time makes sense is if they do business with you. Otherwise, it was a complete waste of time. We call this internal struggle: Cognitive Dissonance. To resolve this conflict, they continue to talk to you, attempting to find a way they can do business with you as the resolution. Keep them talking. Make a follow-up appointment. Find yet another reason to reach out to them. One way or another, get them committed to spending more time, more effort, and even more money during the negotiations, and they will be more inclined to continue with the talks and even close with a deal that was less favorable to them, because once they have gone that far, they will continue to justify to do so. The more time and resources they spend in your direction, the more likely they are to get to the closing table! Thus, **Newton's First Law**.

Newton's second and third laws encompass the emotional side of conflict management, and I will address them together. Most people, when faced with an irate person, believe the best and most effective action is to calm them. Meet their aggression with soft, slow language patterns to calm them down. (And when the force, mass times acceleration, is so overwhelming for you, stepping out of the way or calming them is still the best-case option.) However, there are personality types who will see this as a sign of weakness and steamroll right over you. With effective strength and power, "stand your ground" and **Match Their Energy**.

When you meet FORCE with an equal and opposite force (Newton's third law), you will make them up. You will shift their energy (called a state change) and earn respect all in one motion. They will pause and lower their emotional state as you do. The keys to this technique are 1) confidence and strength in facing off with them (no flinching) and 2) lowering your guard immediately after to lead the way for them to do the same. Once this happens, all future conflicts between the two of you will be resolved through mutual respect established in the stand-off.

One of the easiest to use of the psychological maneuvers you should perfect to create the best momentum in all your negotiations: **Shock and Awe.** Let's assume you listened to my advice and you made sure they said the opening number to be negotiated. I don't care how ridiculous or how sane the number offer is. Your only reaction: SHOCK AND AWE! Become the most over-the-top actor you have ever seen. Be outraged at the number. Express utter shock that they would have the audacity to offer such a ridiculous amount. Say things like, "WOW, really? That's a bold number, don't you think?" or "You really want me to respond to this?" This reaction will break their rhythm, make them rethink, and frame you as someone not easily pushed around. It sets the tone for the rest of the negotiations. It reinforces your position that you can easily walk away from making anything happen.

As you are now in the process of going back and forth with offer and counter-offer in the negotiations, you will be in a position to give and receive concessions. How you approach this stage of negotiations could make or break a deal. In **real estate negotiations**, a **concession** is any **voluntary compromise, accommodation, or give-back** offered by one party to move the deal forward or secure agreement.

Concessions can come in many forms, but they are always about **value exchange**—giving something up to get something else in return. They are deliberate adjustments in price, terms, or conditions made by a buyer or seller to facilitate agreement in a negotiation. First rule of concessions: **Give/Take ALWAYS**. When you give a concession, ask for one in return. You will give up less, and the other side will learn to stop asking. (To stay in control of any negotiations, be the one to set the pace. Be the leader.) Next: Most people negotiate big issues first. Don't. **Start small. Nibble at minor concessions**: a faster close, a repair credit, an extra inspection. These feel harmless to the other party. But once they've given up ten small things, their ground shrinks. Later, when you approach the big task, they've already surrendered much of what they could have given up to get more, in other words, their leverage. You've shaped the battlefield before the main fight even got going. Remember, **Nibble Now, Strike Later.**

    Isolate and Set Aside is another strategy that will serve you at this stage of negotiations. As you approach negotiations, you will want to identify all the components of the deal: Timeline of each stage of the deal, price, contract sign date, close date, financial terms, assets being transferred, and other relevant details. You also want to identify where the line is for you and what you are willing to give up as a concession to get something back.

Click here for a List of your points of negotiations in RE
https://www.NegotiationDomination.com/NegotiationPoints

    Know your **Points of Negotiation**. Most people think price is the only battlefield. Wrong. In real estate, you can negotiate:

- Concessions
- Who pays closing costs
- What stays in the house
- Access for inspection

NOW the fun begins. **Divide and conquer** is the key here. Separating each of the pieces so that you can isolate them in their own micro-negotiations. The person on the other side of the table will want to bundle for power. Concept is for them: "Here are all the things I need to get, at least some of which are required for this deal to go through". WHEN you isolate an item like a close date, both sides go back and forth, eventually coming up with a compromised date. Since it was isolated, they didn't have the option to bundle it with something else and create a give/take scenario. Here is what this might look like: Seller: "Price is too low, and we want to close sooner." Buyer: "If we could, let's set the price aside for a moment and discuss when you want to close. What is the challenge with the date we proposed?" This weakens their position. Instead of attacking both issues at once and using one as leverage, you disarmed them. Later, you will go back to negotiating price, but only after the close date is established and agreed to (assuming that is a contingency that is important to you). When the closing date is established, take it off the table. Buyer: "Now that we have established the when, why don't we take a look at a price we can both agree on?" (Recognize that with this strategy, you can always bundle the price into the negotiations at a later time (when it is advantageous to YOU to do so)).

While we are talking about concessions, let's discuss the effective methodology for navigating negotiations. When we are negotiating price, for instance, most people fall into predictable patterns of behavior that end up 1) giving away their next move(s) and 2) giving up more than needed. Let's say you placed an offer of $550,000, and the seller counters at $590,000. You might counter with $570,000 (Split the Difference). The back and forth might go like that until you settle at somewhere around $580,000, with your go-to strategy being **"Split the Difference"** (which they will quickly recognize). Next time, enact the **Diminishing Concessions** strategy. Start with a tighter counteroffer and adjust it to be a series of diminishing returns. Your first counteroffer could be $557,300, second $561,700, etc. This translates to multiple messages: 1) unpredictability, they do not see an exact pattern, other than the difference is getting smaller (which leads to) 2) they are running out of room. You are willing to give up less and less, which creates a feeling of urgency and scarcity. This will move them to second-guess their position and reinforce that YOU are in control of where this lands.

Dump the Monkey: There's a dangerous illusion in real estate—a mental trap that even seasoned real estate professionals fall into. It happens right after the contract is signed. The ink is still fresh, but your mind has already fast-forwarded to the victory lap. Imagine it: You've finally put the property on the market after months of hesitation. You've had showings, rejections, tire kickers, and now, at last, someone has stepped up. A buyer. A contract. A number you're happy with. You exhale. You call your family. You text your partner. "We did it." You go out to dinner. You might even mentally allocate the money—pay off a credit card here, book that vacation there, reinvest a chunk into your next project. The money feels real because the deal feels done.

But it's not. That's where the psychological trap lies—**counting the money before it hits your account**. It's not greed. It's hope. Anticipation. Relief. But when you start planning your future around a deal that hasn't closed, you set yourself up for emotional free fall.

As the buyer, you are now in the driver's seat. Within two weeks of signing the contracts, you get the inspection report. It has line after line of items that need fixing, with a BIG number at the bottom of the page (when done effectively) as to how much it will take to FIX all this. Don't get anxious. This is their worry to worry about. You take the paperwork, which is essentially an invoice, to the sellers and drop it in their laps. No words. No explanation. Just the inspection report in all its glory. You just DUMPED the MONKEY.

And just like that... their celebration screeches to a halt.

The sellers flip through the document, and it feels like a horror story: roof issues, foundation cracks, outdated wiring, that leaky pipe they" thought" was fixed. Suddenly, they are not imagining profits. They are calculating repair costs. Fear kicks in. "Are they going to back out?" "Do they expect me to fix all this?" "I can't afford this."

Now they are spiraling out of control; Emotionally and mentally. They feel ambushed. They start bracing for the worst. And then, right when they are on edge, you (or your agent call. "We're still interested... we just want a few things addressed."

The seller, upon hearing these words, is so relieved that they are willing to give almost anything to save the deal. They may act angry. They may even push away for a time. However, when the dust settles, they WILL navigate it strategically and give you the world. Here's the truth: They want to keep whatever money they can rather than lose everything (including losing face). As you **Reframe the moment** for them, they begin to see a door, a way out. And they will take it. You say, "Let's separate the cosmetic from the critical. I understand the inspection was thorough, and I'm open to reasonable solutions. I believe these items are critical, and I would need a credit to fix them once I purchase the building."

Recognize that most sellers, in that moment of crisis, give up out of fear. You retain power. You protect your profit. And you move the deal forward.

The best deals are rarely clean. They're built in the messy middle—between excitement and panic, between logic and fear. Be ready.

Remember, this is a psychological engagement, which means there are layers and levels of communication that are happening that you (and certainly others) are not conscious of. A couple of techniques you can implement that directly tap into this unconscious level of engagement.

In negotiation—especially in real estate—**Seeding and Anchoring** are two of the most powerful psychological strategies a Maverick negotiator can deploy. Used effectively, they shape the conversation before it even begins, allowing you to steer the other party's expectations, emotions, and perceived value in your favor.

Seeding is the art of planting ideas early, subtle suggestions that influence how the other party frames the situation. It's about introducing concepts, emotions, or perceived norms in advance of your actual offer so that when the time comes, your proposal feels reasonable, even expected. For example, a buyer might casually mention that homes in the area are often discounted due to aging systems or market shifts, creating a mental benchmark in the seller's mind. Similarly, an investor might seed the value of a fast, cash closing by stating, "My team usually moves fast with sellers who prioritize certainty over squeezing every dollar." These remarks seem like harmless commentary, but they're strategically shaping what's to come.

Anchoring, on the other hand, is about being the first to set the tone numerically or structurally. Whoever throws out the first number often controls the negotiation zone. In real estate, that might look like a buyer saying, "We're ready to move quickly at $295K," even if the asking price was $325K. The seller may counter, but the conversation is now framed within a lower range. Anchoring works because people unconsciously adjust their expectations around the first solid figure or standard they hear. Anchoring can apply not just to price, but to terms, timelines, and contingencies. Done with confidence and backed by logic or third-party validation—like comps or inspection reports—it shifts the frame of reference.

The real power lies in combining the two. First, **seed the idea** gently: what the market expects, what similar deals look like, or what value you bring beyond just money. Then, **anchor with clarity and confidence**: a firm offer or proposal that lands exactly where you wanted it to—already cushioned by the ideas you've seeded. When you master both techniques, you're not reacting to negotiations—you're orchestrating them.

Another powerful psychological tool in negotiation is the use of **Open Loops**—a technique rooted in storytelling, curiosity, and tension. An open loop is when you introduce an idea, question, or promise that remains unresolved, pulling the other party's attention forward and keeping them emotionally engaged until closure is provided. It taps into a natural human desire for completion, making it a subtle but highly effective way to maintain control and influence in the conversation.

In real estate negotiations, this might sound like: "There's something about this property I haven't mentioned yet that could impact value significantly—but let's come back to that in a moment." Or, "We've got a unique financing option that most sellers never see—depending on how our numbers align, I may be able to share it with you." These open-ended remarks keep the other party mentally and emotionally invested, eager to learn more, and more likely to stay at the table, even when objections or friction arise.

Open loops are also powerful when used across multiple touchpoints. If you're negotiating across a series of meetings or calls, ending with an unresolved thought—"There's one more term we're exploring that could make this a no-brainer for both sides"—keeps anticipation alive and positions you as someone with strategic options they need to hear. Combined with seeding and anchoring, open loops amplify your presence and make your proposals feel more compelling. Instead of pushing for a close, you're pulling them toward it, leaving them leaning in, not backing away.

In the world of negotiation, especially in real estate, closing isn't a single moment. It's a series of strategic maneuvers that build psychological momentum toward an inevitable yes. Additionally, understanding people isn't a soft skill in this process. It's your **sharpest weapon**.

Anchoring Effect is also used as a term to describe the mental anchor an initial number has on the psyche. Whatever the first number mentioned is, that becomes the number all others are compared to. When you want to buy a home for $450K, your initial offer should be at $420K. That number becomes the lens through which the seller evaluates everything, making your actual target look reasonable, even generous. Anchoring is a Jedi mind trick every Maverick must master.

I often will float an idea called a **Trial Balloon**. "What if we offered $440K?" It's not a commitment; it's a test. I didn't say I was going to offer $440. I said, "What if I offered you $440k. It gauges reactions and surfaces objections without locking you in. A trial balloon is a soft probe that reveals hard truths before they cost you leverage.

Techniques like **Trial Balloons**, **Seeding** and **Anchoring,** shape the perception of value long before numbers hit the table. At the same time, **Open Loops** keep the other party mentally engaged and leaning in. The **Columbo Close** slides in that final win just when their guard is down. Add to this arsenal techniques like the **Trial Close** (testing the waters before the final ask), the **Assumptive Close** (speaking as if the deal is already done), and the **Takeaway Close** (threatening to remove the offer, increasing urgency and desire), and you become more than just a deal-maker—you become a deal orchestrator. Each of these tactics works because they tap into core human psychology: the need for autonomy, the fear of missing out, the desire for completion, and the comfort of perceived control. Master these closes, and you'll stop hoping for deals to go your way—and start engineering outcomes that do.

CHAPTER FOUR

The Negotiation Dance

Welcome to the center stage of every negotiation, which has an unspoken rhythm - what I call **The Dance**. Just like in ballroom dancing, someone leads and someone follows. And whether you realize it or not, you're constantly teaching the other side how to engage with you—by the **speed**, **tone**, **medium**, and **pattern** of your communication. The key is to be intentional about your role in that dance. Because when you control the tempo, you control the tension. And when you control the tension, you control the outcome. This is where most people believe the negotiation begins, even though, as a Maverick, you now know it started long before this moment. Still, the back-and-forth, the volleying of offers, objections, concessions, and rebuttals—this is where things heat up.

If you want to **slow the negotiation down**—perhaps to create pressure, signal disinterest, or buy time—simply **pause**. Let an email sit. Wait a day or two before responding. Don't reply to texts instantly. This subtle delay communicates power, detachment, and importance. It triggers the other side to lean in, follow up, and chase. On the flip side, if you want to **accelerate the deal**, respond in seconds. Be "always available," rapid-fire with replies and solutions. Suddenly, they're matching your pace, and urgency builds. Either way, your rhythm becomes their rhythm.

Even the **medium** matters. Sending a formal email sets a different tone than a quick text or a personal call. Choosing a phone call instead of email puts you in control of your vocal tone and pace. Setting meetings instead of trading endless back-and-forth messages gives you a structured framework for momentum. You're not just negotiating the deal—you're **teaching them how to negotiate with you**.

The Dance is about more than the words—it's about how and when you deliver them. And once you realize you're leading that dance, you'll stop reacting and start directing. With every beat, every pause, and every step, you subtly guide them toward your desired conclusion, without them even realizing you choreographed the entire thing.

But don't confuse movement with progress. The Dance is not about reacting; it's about leading. Just like in ballroom dancing, someone must guide the rhythm, the pace, and the direction. If you're not leading, you're following. In negotiation, followers lose.

Next:
Some of the basics

In setting the pace and style of the negotiations, you must lead. Standard operating procedure from now on is that **EVERY offer is in writing**. It can initially be verbal when you are in the moment; however, by the end of the day, you re-offer in writing to ensure accuracy. This is your choreography. Your written offer controls the pace. It becomes the reference point, the agenda, and the anchor. People perceive what is written as more real, more final, more legitimate. This is especially useful when you want to steer the conversation back on track. When emotions run high or things get cloudy, simply point to the paper: "Let's come back to the terms we already agreed on."

When at all possible (and since you are in control, it is always possible) **SPEAK LAST. "He who speaks FIRST loses."** Every time you have the opportunity to state a number or a negotiation term, STOP. Wait. Let them talk first. This does two things: First, it gives you more information. Second, it forces them to reveal their position without you bidding against yourself. I have been in deal after deal after deal where the number initially presented was ALREADY better than I anticipated. The one who speaks first often gives up ground unnecessarily and "loses."

Which leads into the next words of advice: PLEASE NEVER NEVER NEVER accept the first offer. Or more specifically, **REJECT FIRST** (even when it is better than you expected and you would be willing to close at that number). The best negotiations are those where both parties walk away feeling good. Even though I am presenting strategies to "win" the negotiations, it doesn't mean the other side has to FEEL like they lost. When you accept the FIRST offer (or counteroffer), the opposing side automatically thinks, This was too easy. I could have done better. Make the WIN more satisfying for them by making them fight for it. YES - **Speak Last/Reject First.**

The Decoy

Sometimes the most powerful strategy in the negotiation isn't what you ask for—it's what you pretend to care about. That's the essence of the Decoy.

Let's break it down: you deliberately introduce a demand that appears crucial to you—tight timeline, extra furniture, closing location, anything really—only to later "give it up" in exchange for a true win that matters most to your bottom line. It's the art of the strategic sacrifice.

Say you start off demanding a 7-day close. You act firm about it. You posture. You even threaten to walk away. Then, when the other party pushes back, you "reluctantly" concede to a 30-day close... but in exchange for a $10,000 price reduction.

Here's the kicker: you never cared about the timeline. That wasn't your goal. Your goal was the money, and now you have it.

The power of the Decoy is that it creates a false battleground. You let them fight and win on terrain you never planned to defend. This leaves them feeling victorious, and you walking away with exactly what you wanted.

Use this when:

- You anticipate resistance to your true objective.
- You want to create goodwill while still winning.
- You need to give something up, but don't want it to cost you.

Pro tip: Always set up your Decoy as non-negotiable at first. The stronger your "attachment," the more valuable the trade when you let it go.

Goodwill Negotiation

Most amateurs think kindness in negotiation is a weakness. Pros know—it's a tactical weapon. Welcome to the realm of Goodwill Negotiation. In this move, you offer a small gesture of goodwill, like agreeing to fix a minor plumbing issue, covering inspection costs, or giving the seller flexibility on move-out. It's not just a nice thing to do. It is a calculated, high-ROI play to build trust, disarm skepticism, and flip resistance into cooperation.

Why does it work? Because people are hardwired to reciprocate. When you go first with a favor, they feel compelled to give something back—whether it's a lower price, quicker paperwork, or removing a contingency.

Here's how a Maverick plays this: Let's say a seller is dragging their feet on a response. You say, "Look, I want this to work for both of us. I'll cover that $300 clean-up from the inspection." Instantly, the tone changes. You've become a problem-solver, not a predator. Now, they're more likely to counter with a meaningful concession, like dropping the price or closing sooner. You've just rebalanced the entire emotional energy of the deal.

Use this when:

- Trust is low and tension is high.
- You want to shift from adversary to ally.
- You're about to make a bigger ask and need to soften the field.

Power move: Always tie your goodwill to timing. "I'll take care of that if we can sign today." It becomes a catalyst, not a giveaway.

Once you've set the rhythm of the negotiation through The Dance, it's time to step into one of the most nuanced parts of any deal—**pricing**. This is where the real tension lives, and where mastery lies in subtlety. When you're at the edge of a number or pushing for better terms, you use techniques like **Test the Line**, **Rounding and Reframing**, and the strategic power of **silence** to guide the outcome without direct confrontation.

Start with the **Test the Line** technique. This is about boldness followed by stillness. You throw out a number that challenges their position, lower than they want, harder than they expect. Then you pause. Look them in the eye. No backpedaling, no nervous chatter. Just hold. Their reaction tells you everything: Did they flinch? Did they hesitate? Did they get defensive—or curious? That moment of discomfort is your edge. If you've gone too far, you'll feel it—and you can pull back. But if not? You push again. Test it one more time. For example, if a seller says, "I won't take a penny less than $340,000," you reply: "So just to be clear—if I offered you $335,000 in cash today, I should walk away and not waste your time?" That's a line they've drawn. Now you're finding out if it's real or just a bluff.

Then comes the **Rounding and Reframing** strategy. If they quote $13,459, you reply, "Sounds like you're at $13K and change. Would $11K be acceptable?" Without a fight, you just shaved off $459. And if they push back, you reframe, "Okay, so it sounds like $13K is your true number, then?" Now you have clarity and control. The same applies to ranges. If they say, "Our budget is between $3K and $5K," don't meet them in the middle—start at the bottom: "$3K is a little higher than we anticipated." You've reframed the entire conversation around the low end of their range. On the flip side, if a buyer says, "We were hoping to spend around $2,500," you say, "Most of our clients invest between $3,000 and $5,000, so you're right in the ballpark." Now $5K feels like the top of a reasonable range rather than a stretch.

One additional powerhouse move: **Odd Numbers Magic.** Ever notice in all the major chains throughout the country, all the prices end in a "5", '7", or "9"? This isn't random. All the studies have shown people respond more positively to these numbers at the end of a price. It "feels" smaller to them.

The details of why are here for you to explore
https://www.NegotiationDomination.com/Psychologyof pricing

With this being the case, why wouldn't all of your offers end in a 5,7, or 9? Yes - Literally use ODD Numbers to win the day.

One other way to use ODD Number Magic. Use odd (strange) numbers. Imagine you are placing an offer on a property, and the offer is $673,973 vs. the usual $670,000 or $675,000. What do you believe the receiver of this offer is thinking? Either you are nuts, or it's another strategy in negotiations that works (no one can predict what a crazy person is going to do). OR you have really worked these numbers, which throws off their usual thought process for negotiation. It psychologically restricts the magnitude of the difference between the counteroffer and the original. Game on! Your next offer... Use Odd Number Magic to get an edge right off the bat.

And through it all, never underestimate the power to **Shut Up**. Once you've made your offer, stop. Don't explain. Don't justify. Don't soften the blow. Just sit in the silence. Let it linger. Most people hate the discomfort and will rush to fill the void, often with concessions, compromises, or clues about their real limits. When you're silent, you're in control. You've already danced them to the edge of decision; now let the quiet push them over. Pricing is emotional. Your job is to keep them in motion. Test. Reframe. Round. Pause. And when the time is right, say less because the most powerful negotiator isn't always the one who speaks last. It's the one who doesn't need to.

There's an advanced layer to the **Shut-Up** technique that few ever master, but those who do win bigger and more often. It's not just about creating silence. It's about creating **space** for your offer, your ask, or your bold statement to **linger**. That pause isn't empty—it's loaded. You're giving them the emotional runway to feel the weight of what you just said. To process it. To wrestle with it. And ultimately, to respond.

But here's the kicker: it's not just your **words** that need to go still—your **body** does too. Any movement—shifting in your seat, a nervous smile, a raised brow, even leaning forward—can break the spell. It disrupts their processing and gives away your own tension. Just like a sudden comment can defuse pressure, so can a twitch of the body. So when you deliver your line—"I can close in 7 days, as-is, at $275K..."—**stop everything**. Your words, your hands, your face, your breath. Go still. Stay present. Stay neutral. Let the tension sit in the room like a heavy fog.

Watch them. Wait. And here's the Maverick rule: **you don't move until they do**. When they shift, speak, or react, that's your signal that the silence has done its job. Now you can re-engage. But until then, you're the statue at the center of the storm. Calm. In control. And commanding the dance with nothing but presence. This is negotiation at its highest level—not through force, but through stillness. Let your silence—and your stillness—say everything.

CHAPTER FIVE

Always Question

In the world of real estate negotiation—and sales at large—there's one weapon that separates the amateurs from the pros. It's not your pitch. It's not your offer. It's not your slick presentation or flashy close. It's your **question**. Questions aren't just tools—they're weapons. In the hands of an effective negotiator, questions shape perception, shift power, and unlock the hidden doors inside every negotiation. If you want to control the frame, uncover objections, and guide the outcome, it doesn't start with making statements. It starts with asking better questions.

The most effective negotiators don't talk more. They ask more. They don't sell harder. They uncover deeper. And they don't push—they pull the truth out of the other person until the path to closing is obvious and frictionless.

Most people think selling is about convincing. It's not. Selling—especially in high-stakes real estate—is about discovering. It's a guided excavation of **motivation, fears, priorities, timelines**, and **personal beliefs**. The more you know, the more power you hold. And the only way to truly know anything in a negotiation is to ask. Statements push. Questions pull. And when you pull people in the right direction, they believe it was their idea all along. That's how deals get closed. People will tell you everything you need to close them—if you know how to ask the right questions and shut up long enough to listen.

Most People Don't Ask Enough Questions, or in too many cases, ANY questions. WHY? Here's the dirty little truth: most salespeople are afraid. They fear looking stupid. They fear sounding unprepared. They fear losing control. They fear awkward silence. So instead of asking questions, they talk. They pitch. They explain. They overload. But here's what they don't realize: every moment they're talking, they're not learning. And if they're not learning, they're negotiating in the dark.

The irony? The more questions you ask, the more control you actually gain. Because the one asking the questions controls the direction of the conversation. YES - The one asking the questions IS the one controlling the conversation.

Questions shift the mental state of your prospect. They force engagement. They bypass defenses. They redirect your attention from fear to focus; From insecure to inquisitive. And most importantly, they allow your prospect to convince themselves. Realize, as you are asking questions, your receiver will be looking for the answers. With the most effective questions, those answers will lead them right to you. They will literally sell themselves.

One of the most underrated tools in a negotiator's arsenal is the **Trial Close**. This question feels harmless but reveals everything. Unlike a full close, a trial close doesn't ask for the final decision. It checks alignment, tests readiness, and exposes hidden objections before they derail the deal. And in real estate—where emotions run high, stakes are real, and timing is everything—**trial closes keep you from walking blind into resistance**.

The beauty of a trial close is that it invites conversation, not confrontation. It lets you gauge whether your prospect is on board without applying pressure. You're not asking "Will you accept the offer?" You're asking, "If everything looked right, is this the kind of offer that would make sense for you?" Subtle. Safe. Smart. And when you ask it well, their answer tells you exactly what's holding them back—or moves them forward.

You must use trial closes early and often.

Most salespeople think they lose deals because they didn't have the perfect pitch or didn't overcome the right objection. But in truth, most deals are lost for a much simpler reason: they didn't ask enough questions.

In a standard 30 to 60 minute sales conversation, the average salesperson asks maybe three to six questions in total. Add to that low number the fact that most of them are checklist questions at best. "What's your budget?" "When do you want to move?" "Have you worked with a realtor before?" Surface-level stuff. Harmless, yes. But useless when it comes to true discovery. After that, they talk. And talk. And talk. Explaining features, sharing data, presenting offers—guessing, not knowing. It's a monologue in disguise.

The most effective negotiators flip that script completely. Instead of trying to persuade, they investigate. Instead of guessing, they dig. A true professional will ask 12 to 20 meaningful questions for a single conversation. That means every 2 to 3 minutes, they're re-engaging the prospect, deepening the dialogue, and peeling back the layers of motivation, fear, and desire. They're not just asking more questions—they're asking better ones.

The right question at the right time unlocks everything. It reveals the real reason they're hesitating. It shows you exactly what they need to hear next. It allows you to tailor your solution in a way that feels like it was built just for them. Most importantly, it invites the prospect to talk themselves into the deal, in their own words, on their own terms.

You don't need to close harder. You need to ask smarter. Rotate through discovery questions, motivator questions, trial closes, tie-downs, and objection-revealers. Ask about their timelines, their fears, and their "whys." Then keep asking. And when they ask you a question, answer it with another question. Not to be evasive—but to go deeper.

Because in this game, the one who asks the most doesn't just stay in control; they walk away with the deal every time.

The power of the **trial close**: asking a question that feels safe but reveals deep commitment. Some examples might be:

- "If everything looked good and you felt comfortable with the terms, is there any reason you wouldn't move forward?"
- "If this checked all the boxes, how soon would you want to make a move?"
- "Does this feel like something you could say yes to if the numbers made sense?"

"What would need to change for this to feel like the right fit?

These aren't pitches—they're **discovery**

accelerators. You're testing the waters, checking the temperature, and guiding the prospect without pressure. And every time they give you an answer, they're telling you what it will take to get them across the finish line. Some other categories you should explore with questions:

- **Discovery Questions**: "What's prompting this sale now?"
- **Motivator Questions**: "How will this change your day-to-day life?"
- **Trial Closes**: "Does this feel like a move in the right direction?"
- **Tie-Downs**: "That kind of speed would give you peace of mind, wouldn't it?"
- **Objection-Revealers**: "What's the one thing still holding you back?"
- **Decision Qualifiers**: "Is there anyone else involved in making the final call?"
- **Power Questions**: "Why is this important to you now?"

These questions will do the heavy lifting. They bring up objections before they grow roots. They help you adjust your approach in real time BEFORE it is too late. More importantly, they turn the prospect from a passive listener into an active participant: someone who starts talking themselves into the deal.

With trial closes, you're not asking for the finish line—you're simply making sure you're still on the right track. And when you master the art of checking in without backing down, you never get blindsided by a "no" because you saw it coming, handled it early, and paved the way to yes.

Trial Closes/TieDowns

https://www.NegotiationDomination.com/TrialclosesTieDowns

Add to this another powerhouse questioning tool: **Tie Downs!** Tie-downs are short phrases or questions added to the end of a statement that subtly create agreement. They sound innocent, but they're psychological pressure points that build "yes momentum."

Examples:

- "That would make things easier for you, wouldn't it?"
- "You want to avoid all the inspection drama, right?"
- "That kind of peace of mind is worth acting quickly, don't you think?"

Each tie-down is a mini-close. String a few together, and by the time you make your actual offer, the only logical answer is yes. Tie-downs reinforce alignment. They are the **emotional glue,** and when used alongside the right questions, they lock in the deal.

A couple of final notes on questions. Learn to ASK – Don't Assume! Too many negotiators make fatal assumptions that hold you back or kill the opportunity of a deal in its tracks. They believe without asking, "They can't go lower.", "They probably won't agree to that.", "They'll never say yes to this." The truth is, you don't know until you ask. Assumptions kill deals. Curiosity creates them. Ask with intention. Ask with consistency. Ask until you know.

ASK WHY! The best question that every 3-year-old knows all too well. This one question opens up nearly every closed mind.

- "Why do you need that timeline?"
- "Why is that number important to you?"

Why digs deeper than what or how. Why peels back the surface and gets to the story. It makes people think. It makes them explain. And when they explain, they expose leverage. The question "why" forces introspection. It reveals motivation. It cracks open objections. And it makes the client say the things they need to hear themselves say in order to move forward. Don't be afraid to dig. Prospects respect depth. They crave being heard and understood. And when you ask why—not in judgment, but in curiosity—you elevate yourself from salesperson to trusted advisor.

Why is especially effective when you hit resistance. Instead of pushing back, simply ask: **"Why is that a dealbreaker for you?"** You'll be amazed at how quickly that wall crumbles.

NOW the technique that you will resist, that will be uncomfortable at first, and yet will be the power play. Never answer a question directly!

Wait? What? Paul, we were trained our whole life to answer a question with an answer; the more direct, the better. If we did not answer directly to our teachers or our parents, we were punished one way or another. What are you saying?

Every time you are asked a question, do not answer it. Ask a question in return. This will keep you effectively in control of the conversation and the negotiation process. For example, if someone asks, "What's your best price?" You don't answer. Instead, you ask:

- "Are you asking that because you're ready to make a decision today?"
- "What price were you hoping to hear?"

- "If I give you that number and it works for you, what happens next?"

Each question peels back another layer and gives you more information for leverage later. When you answer too soon, you give away power. But when you **respond with a question**, you retain control, shift the pressure, and gain valuable insight. Remember, **knowledge is power.** The way to gain that power is by asking.

The ultimate power question I refer to as the **"Columbo Close"**. One of the most underestimated yet highly effective negotiation techniques is the Columbo Close, also known as the "Oh, by the way…" close—named after the famous TV detective Lieutenant Columbo. In every episode, just as the suspect thought they were off the hook and the conversation was wrapping up, Columbo would pause, scratch his head, and say, "Oh, just one more thing…" then deliver the line that cracked the whole case wide open. In negotiation, this same move can work wonders.

The Columbo Close is used right at the end of the deal, when everyone thinks everything's already been decided. The tension has dropped, the walls are down, and the other party has mentally celebrated. That's when you lean in and casually drop your final ask:

"Oh, by the way… would you mind covering the closing costs?"

or

"Oh, just one more thing… could we leave the appliances?"

It works because psychologically, people hate backtracking once they feel they've already agreed to something. It's easier for them to say yes to a small, final request than to reopen the negotiation altogether. Their desire to stay in agreement, keep the good feeling going, and avoid rocking the boat works in your favor.

The key is in the delivery—it must feel casual, not calculated. Like it just popped into your mind, not like it was part of your master plan all along (even though, of course, it was). Use it at the end of an offer, a meeting, or even while signing paperwork. Done right, the Columbo Close lets you squeeze out one last concession or win, without resistance and without triggering a defensive response. It's polite, unexpected, and devastatingly effective.

Most deals are lost not because you didn't have the right pitch, but because you didn't ask the right questions. The truth is that control doesn't come from dominating the conversation; it comes from directing it through curiosity, strategy, and silence. Ask deeper. Ask more often. Ask smarter. And when in doubt? Ask again. Because the greatest closers in the world are not the ones with the most charisma; they're the ones with the most questions.

Get the full glossary of RE and Sales terms:
https://www.NegotiationDomination.com/Glossary

CHAPTER SIX

Leverage Strategies
How to Tilt the Field

Power in negotiation is rarely loud. It's not in shouting, pounding the table, or strong-arming your way through. That kind of force might win a moment, but it rarely wins the deal. Real power is quiet. Subtle. Invisible. It's not in what you demand, but in what they believe. **Power is positioning**—the carefully curated perception that they need you more than you need them. And that perception is built on leverage.

Leverage is the art of making your smallest assets feel like your biggest strengths. It's not about overwhelming force—it's about emotional gravity. A well-timed pause. A piece of data they didn't expect. A soft suggestion with hard implications. A walk-away that signals, "You're about to lose something valuable."

When you master leverage, you stop hoping for power. You walk into every negotiation knowing you already have it. You created the opportunity. Manifested the scenario. You built it long before the conversation ever began.

The most reliable source of leverage is **knowledge**—what you know that they don't (or what you know that they don't know you know). Information is influential. In real estate, this starts with the basics: the comps, the neighborhood, the seller's timeline, the buyer's financial pressure, the competing offers, and the zoning laws. But true leverage isn't just knowing more. It's knowing what they think they know, and being prepared to dismantle it.

I once sat across from a seller convinced their home was worth $800K. They cited a sale two streets over. What they missed was that the other house had 900 more square feet, a pool, and backed up to a golf course. I slid the comps across the table and said, "I figured you'd want the real data." No need to argue. The facts did the lifting. We closed at $695K.

When you have the knowledge edge, you become more than a negotiator. You become the authority. Authority, in turn creates trust, credibility, and leverage.

Another form of subtle power comes from what you're willing to give, strategically. That's where the **loss leader** comes in. This is where you make a sacrifice that looks generous, but in reality, sets the stage for a bigger win. It could be a flexible closing date that buys you a massive price reduction, covering their moving costs in exchange for seller financing and agreeing to cosmetic repairs to avoid them demanding a structural inspection. These aren't concessions. They are negotiation plays. You have successfully positioned the deal to be exactly where you want it. Before you walk into your next deal, create a list of all the concessions you are willing to give up that would mean more to them than it would to you. One or all of these could be your loss leaders that you use to get a bigger (or more valuable) concession in exchange.

Sometimes the most effective leverage is not in winning the whole war at once, but in stacking small victories. This is the essence of the **Minor Point Close**. Instead of aiming for the full commitment, you ask for something easy: "Can we at least agree on the inspection period?" or "Would you be open to including the appliances if we move forward today?" Each small yes lowers resistance. It creates a psychological rhythm—agree, agree, agree—and by the time you ask for the big yes, you have already trained them to give it. The conclusion feels natural because it's built one layer at a time.

As the deal nears its conclusion, a new form of leverage emerges: **the finish line**. People hate quitting near the end. They don't want to feel like their effort was wasted. (They don't want to experience Cognitive Dissonance.) They don't want to start over. This is where **Finish Line Framing** kicks in. Phrases like, "We've come this far. I'd hate to see it fall apart over one detail," or "Everything else is locked in. Let's just close this up,". These statements help to keep the momentum going. You are showing them the edge of the finish line, and most people will sprint across it rather than retreat. Use this tendency to your advantage.

But sometimes, things stall. Tension builds. They push too far. That's when the most powerful play isn't to push. It is to pull. Time for the **Takeaway Close**. You say, "Maybe this isn't the right time." Or, "We might not be the right buyer for this." Or the simple, cutting: "I understand. I think we are going to go with another option." Suddenly, they're not negotiating anymore. They are panicking. The deal they thought was safe just vanished. The brain hates loss more than it loves gain. The fear of missing out (FOMO) kicks in. When you threaten (or even hint at) walking away, you force them to decide: Do they want to lose this deal, or do they want to give you what you want?

The Take Away close is a powerhouse psychological tool, and more often than not, **they chase you to give you everything you want... on your terms**. I once used this technique in buying a car AFTER all the paperwork was signed. They had attempted to pass off a vehicle to me that was different from what they told me I was getting. In these situations, you MUST stay strong. You MUST stay focused. You MUST be willing to lose the deal entirely! I was determined to get what I wanted or walk. They let the deal unravel to the point of undoing all the paperwork, deleting all the files that had already been done, and refunding me the deposit I had already paid. My hand was on the door of the dealership, about to leave. YES - they waited to the very second (I guess they didn't believe I was really going to leave. They don't know me.) They ended up finding what I wanted and even gave me a free rental until everything was resolved. Dare to use the takeaway close... it works.

Now add **time pressure**, **scarcity**, and **competition**, and you create an irresistible cocktail of urgency. Offers that expire. Buyers circling. Funds with deadlines. You don't have to lie—you just have to make it clear the opportunity isn't endless. You're not waiting forever. And neither is your lender. That subtle tension makes your offer feel more valuable. Its finite nature creates scarcity as a powerful motivator.

When it's time to explain your terms, tell a story. **Paint a picture**. People don't make decisions based on numbers—they make them based on feeling. And stories trigger feelings. Describe what the deal will do for them. Give them a before-and-after transformation. A seller going from burdened to free. A buyer moving into their dream future. Frame it in outcomes, not features. Make the intangibles (speed, simplicity, peace of mind) feel tangible. Words carry weight, but you can change that weight by **changing the words themselves**. That's the art of **relabeling and reframing**. Don't say "lowball." Say "a conservative offer given the current market." Don't say "we're walking away." Say "we're exploring other options." If they reference a range like "We're looking for $3–5K," you respond, "$3K is a little higher than we anticipated." Suddenly, you're negotiating from the bottom of their range, not the top.

One direct, almost obvious, and simple way to disarm their negotiations. **Label it!** You recognize that a tactic can even identify its author. Call them out on it, "Ah, anchoring. I respect that. Did you learn that from Zig or Tom Hopkins?" Call it out with a smile. You will break their pattern. You will regain control. They can't run a script if you rewrite it mid-sentence. This works like a charm in disrupting their flow and making them self-conscious for the rest of the engagement. Anything that gets them a bit off balance can become a huge advantage.

Another closing strategy that delivers powerful psychological leverage is **The Three Option Offer**. At its core, this technique is rooted in the behavioral principle that **a binary yes/no decision often leads to "no"**, even when the "yes" is a strong option. When people are presented with only one path forward, it triggers resistance. They feel trapped, limited, or like they're being sold—activating skepticism and fear of making the wrong choice.

However, when you expand the decision from one option to **three distinct offers**, something powerful happens. The human brain feels **a sense of control**. It shifts from "Should I do this?" to "Which of these is best for me?" That shift creates ownership of the decision, which increases the likelihood of commitment. Psychologically, people are more likely to say yes when they have the ability to choose the version of yes that fits them best.

In real estate, **The Three Option Offer** becomes a masterstroke of strategy. For example, instead of offering just a flat $300K, a buyer might structure the proposal like this:

1. **Option A:** $295K, close in 14 days, as-is, cash.
2. **Option B:** $310K, 30-day close, with minor repairs requested.
3. **Option C:** $325K, contingent on financing, 60-day close, seller pays closing costs.

Now the seller isn't rejecting a deal—they're choosing which deal they like best. Each option plays on different values: speed, certainty, price, or flexibility. It's a psychological win-win. Even if they choose the middle or highest offer, they feel empowered because they made the choice.

This approach works on the buyer side too. A seller might present:

1. **Option A:** $500K, no contingencies, appliances not included.
2. **Option B:** $515K, includes appliances, close in 30 days.
3. **Option C:** $525K, fully furnished, flexible closing.

In every case, you're framing the conversation with a higher chance of success, not by forcing a "yes," but by giving tailored options that create perceived value and control. The Three Option Offer isn't just about pricing—it's about **positioning** the path to agreement so the answer is always yes.

But perhaps the most overlooked leverage strategy of all lies not in what you say, but in how you say nothing at all. **Your body language can create huge leverage.** Your nonverbal cues carry more weight than most realize. When you deliver your offer, your counter, or your bold move, don't just shut up. **Go still.** No fidgeting. No leaning forward. No smiling nervously. Just eye contact, calm breath, steady hands. Silence backed by stillness creates pressure. Movement breaks the tension. Stay composed, and they'll start squirming in their seat to break the silence for you. Let your facial expression remain neutral. Let your body become a statue. Say everything with your presence and say nothing with your mouth. And here's the Maverick move: **you don't move until they do**. When they shift, speak, or gesture—that's your cue. You've held the frame. Now let them follow it.

Body Language Mastery: Influence Without Saying a Word

In the world of negotiation, your words matter. But they're not the first thing people notice, and they're rarely the most persuasive. Long before you speak, your body has already delivered its message. You walk into the room, and before you've said a word, the other side has made 10 subconscious judgments. Who's in control? Who's confident? Who's chasing? Who's holding power? The reality is, **your body language closes (or loses) more deals than your mouth ever will.**

Influence doesn't begin when you open your mouth; it begins the moment you step into view. Presence is power. You either command the space, or you give it away. And when you want the deal to move in your favor, you need to understand that every gesture, every pause, every shift of weight is either reinforcing your authority or eroding it.

So, how do the best negotiators use body language to influence without saying a word? They move with **intention**. They stay still with **purpose**. They understand that **control isn't loud—it's subtle.** And it starts the moment you walk in the door.

You don't barge into the room. You enter. Deliberately. Calmly. Chin level. Shoulders back. Feet planted. You don't rush to fill the silence. You let it stretch. Because you're not trying to sell them. You're giving them a rare opportunity to do business with you. Use your body in congruence with what you are saying and expressing. For most of the time, you want people to like you and want to be near you. The number one way to do that is SMILE. A smile will come through whether you're talking to somebody on the phone or in person. It is contagious. When you smile, people will smile back. I have trained telemarketers over the years, and one of the first secrets of the trade is to put a mirror right by your phone. When you are going to reach out to a prospect or client, look in the mirror to check that your smile is in place.

One of the most overlooked, underestimated rapport builders in existence is **mirror and matching.** People trust people who feel like them. Not people who look like them. People who move like them. Think like them. Speak at their pace. That's where **mirroring** becomes a psychological gateway.

You don't need to imitate—this isn't mimicry. This is alignment. They lean forward, you lean slightly in. They speak slowly, so you slow down your cadence. They pause after statements; you pause too. Their arms relax at their sides, and yours do the same. No effort, no exaggeration. Just rhythm. Subtle harmony. And once you're in sync, you can lead them where you want to go.

YES. Here is the Maverick move: **match first, then lead.** Because once you've aligned, they'll follow. That's when you raise the energy. That's when you steer the pace. That's when you take control—and they don't even realize you've shifted the dance.

It's not just about mirroring—it's about mastering the few key body language moves that signal leadership without saying a word. Start with the **Freeze After the Offer**. When you drop your number or ask your bold question, freeze. Still your body. Still your breath. Don't blink. Don't fidget. Let the silence land like a weight. Most people rush to fill that silence with explanation or apology. But not you. You let it work for you. You hold the frame.

Use the **Lean-In, Lean-Out Dynamic** with intention. When you want to create closeness, lean in. When you want to assert strength and detachment, lean back. Watch how they react. If they start leaning in when you pull back, that is what we call a buying signal; "a clue".

Keep your **hands open** when you're building trust, palms visible, gestures controlled. When you're making a critical point or asserting value, **steeple your fingers**. This power pose says without words, "I know exactly what I'm doing."

Watch the head tilt. Slight. Intentional. While listening, it signals presence and curiosity. Use it to encourage them to open up. Use it when you want to draw more out of their story. The tilt says, "I'm with you." And they'll give you more if they feel that.

Now, don't just watch yourself, or them. **Consciously read them**. Their bodies are giving up all the secrets.

Feet pointed toward the door? They're not committed. Arms crossed tightly with no movement? They're defending. Quick eye dart and lip bite after you say your price? They flinched. That's your window. That's where the truth lives. People lie with words all the time. Their posture is screaming the truth.

Now, find out whether you're winning. Watch what happens when you shift. Pause. Slow down. If they match your energy, you're leading the dance. If they mirror your nod, you've built rapport. If they hold your eye contact, they're bought in. If they flinch when you test the line, they just showed you their pain point.

That's where your leverage lives; not in louder voices, but in **quieter cues**. When you move with purpose, pause with confidence, hold still at the right moment, and match their rhythm just long enough to lead them back to yours, you become the anchor in the room. You create safety, certainty, and strength. Those are the things that close deals every time.

In the end, leverage is never about pushing harder—it's about positioning smarter. It's the dance of subtle power: knowledge, stories, timing, silence, scarcity, and presence. All working in harmony. All tilting the field without force. Time to tilt it for yourself.

Deadline Pressure

In negotiation, urgency isn't a disadvantage; it's a weapon. When you set a deadline, you're not just drawing a line in the sand; you're shifting the psychological pressure squarely onto the other party.

Saying, "This offer is only good until Friday at 5 PM," immediately reframes the dynamic. Now they're not just evaluating your offer—they're racing against the clock. That time constraint creates scarcity, triggers the fear of missing out (FOMO), and forces decision-making that favors you. When they feel the countdown ticking, logic takes a back seat to urgency, and hesitation turns into action.

This isn't about manipulation—it's about

momentum. If a negotiation stalls, it dies. Deadline Pressure injects adrenaline into the deal, making it real, tangible, and time-bound. Use it whenever you sense hesitation or delay creeping in. Time is leverage. Own the clock, and you own the deal.

Phantom Offer
Want to light a fire under someone's decision-making? Introduce a phantom.

Say this: "We're also considering another property and should be making a decision by tomorrow." Instantly, the entire tone of the negotiation changes. That one sentence subtly tells them, you're not their only option. It introduces scarcity. It creates pressure. It signals that their window to act is closing fast.

Here's the beauty of the Phantom Offer—it doesn't even have to be real. Just the perception of competition is enough to push the other side into action. They start to question their position. They reevaluate their timeline. They even get a little desperate. And in that emotional shift lies your advantage.

Now, use this responsibly. It's not a lie; it's a framing device. Whether it's another property, another investor, or another buyer, it's about keeping the leverage squarely in your court. When they think you've got options, suddenly they start fighting to become your best one.

Leverage Timing
Time is not neutral. It's not passive. It's one of the sharpest tools in the Maverick negotiator's toolbox.
In a seller's market—when homes fly off the shelves—you strike fast, decisively, with strength. You shorten the timeline. You act before the competition does. You create urgency because waiting costs you the deal.

But in a buyer's market—when inventory sits and

sellers sweat—you do the opposite. You drag your feet. You schedule your follow-up for a week later. You let silence ferment. And every tick of the clock makes them more anxious, more motivated, more flexible.

This is Leverage Timing. You're not just responding to the market—you're using it. By adjusting your tempo to the terrain, you control the negotiation environment. If they're hungry for action, delay it. If they're slow to move, accelerate. Let your timing unsettle their comfort zone.

Remember: the one who controls the clock often controls the outcome.

Trade-Offs

Every negotiation is a give-and-take. The amateurs compromise. The Mavericks trade.

A Trade-Off isn't a loss; it's a strategic swap. You give up something low on your priority list to gain something high on theirs. You say, "I'll agree to the full asking price… if you agree to pay the closing costs." Or "I'll accept your inspection terms if you let us extend the financing contingency."

The brilliance of the Trade-Off is this: it feels balanced, but it's weighted in your favor. You engineer wins by exchanging low-cost concessions for high-value advantages. You look collaborative while you're executing a stealth power play.

You never just give something up. Every time you move, you gain. And that, my friend, is negotiation at its finest.

CHAPTER SEVEN

Beyond the Table

Where the Real Negotiation Lives

Most people see negotiation as a one-act play. You sit down, talk it out, shake hands, sign papers, and walk away with the win. But that's just the visible performance. It is the part the amateurs obsess over, and yet it is only part of the story. The truth is, **real negotiation is a multi-act production**, and the most important scenes happen off-stage: before the curtain rises and after the deal has closed.

Those who win consistently, who walk into rooms already positioned as the person to say yes to, understand that what happens before and after the table is where the real leverage is built. They aren't just skilled negotiators. They're strategic operators. And their power doesn't come from their pitch—it comes from the **congruency of who they are and what they portray** that they constructed around every deal.

Let's pull back the curtain and explore the strategies that make-or-break negotiations—not in the moment—but in the momentum surrounding it.

The Home Court Advantage is key.

Control the environment, and you control the energy. When a negotiation happens on your terms, using your contracts, inside your office, or even on your Zoom link, you've already positioned yourself as the leader. There's psychological weight to home court. It signals authority. It suggests preparedness. More importantly, it trains the other party to play by your rules.

Your contracts should reflect your rhythm: your inspection timelines, your preferred contingencies, and your method of closing. Most people will adapt to what's already formatted and pre-filled, because it feels official. You've established what's normal, and they'll often negotiate within that frame instead of challenging it from scratch.

Be aware, I will always look to use my contracts whenever possible, and I will take the lead in providing the contracts every time. I also have a contract I use when I am a buyer and a different contract when I am the seller. Each is designed to give me an edge in terms of safeguards. Also, be aware that if someone else provided the contract, they too designed it to be in their favor. This is where most amateurs fumble. They use someone else's contract, accept someone else's terms, and enter someone else's space. In doing so, they enter someone else's frame. And once you are in someone else's frame, you are already playing at a disadvantage.

Your Digital Presence Is Negotiating for You

These days, the negotiation begins the moment they search your name (which they will all do). Before a seller agrees to meet or a buyer takes your offer seriously, they're researching. They're clicking through your website, checking your socials, scanning your LinkedIn, and Googling your reviews. **Every word, image, and impression become part of the deal before you've even spoken.**

If your online presence is polished, aligned, and professional, you create immediate trust. You walk into the conversation with silent authority. However, be warned. If it's scattered, outdated, or missing altogether? You've already lost ground you didn't know you were standing on. Think of your digital presence as a **pre-frame for power**. It's your opportunity to walk into every room with credibility already working in your favor. A professional headshot, clear messaging, testimonials, and a consistent brand voice say, "I do this. I'm the real deal. You're in good hands." People don't argue with certainty—they respond to it.

Recently, I was at a last-minute dinner with potential new strategic partners. It was, for all intents and purposes, the beginning of our negotiations to do future business together. We were introduced through a third party, and they had not yet looked me up. At dinner, they ended up (yes, positioned by me) looking at my social media platforms. They instantly said, "We didn't know we were sitting with a celebrity. You're pretty important according to these numbers." Positioning on all levels.

Be sure to follow us on social media
https://www.NegotiationDomination.com/Social

Brand Congruency: Align with the Market You Want to Own

It's not enough to look professional. You need to feel aligned with the people you want to attract. If you're working in luxury real estate, but your branding screams discount, your prospects feel the disconnect. On the flip side, if you're negotiating with distressed sellers and your website is dripping in corporate polish, they'll feel like you can't possibly understand their world. That's where **brand congruency** becomes a negotiation weapon. Your message, marketing, and materials should **echo the concerns, dreams, and language** of your target market. When your external brand matches their internal conversation, trust forms instantly. They think, This person gets me. That trust and emotional resonance show up as smoother negotiations, higher conversion, and faster yeses. It's not magic. It's alignment. And it makes everything else easier.

Strategic Positioning Through Relationships

One of the most powerful levers you can have in any negotiation is someone they trust... who already trusts you. When your name is introduced by a mutual contact, a respected figure, or a known authority, the entire dynamic shifts. You're no longer cold. You're vetted. You walk in with borrowed credibility, and the other party's resistance drops by half before you say a word. This is the power of **social leverage**. And it doesn't happen by accident. It's cultivated through intentional networking long before the deal even exists. It's grabbing coffee with the right lenders, supporting local politicians, helping attorneys win, sending leads to agents, and staying top-of-mind in the circles that matter. Strategic relationships aren't just about referrals. They're about positioning. In this game, **who knows you matters just as much as what you know**.

Systems and Follow-Up: The Deal After the Deal

Most people think the close is the end of the road. But the real pros know it's just the beginning of your next negotiation. The way you follow up, handle logistics, and communicate post-close determines your long-term leverage. Did you deliver on what you promised? Did you treat the admin staff with respect? Did your team follow through with clarity and precision? Every piece matters. People remember how you made them feel after the papers were signed. This is where **systems** become a secret weapon. A clean onboarding flow. A templated thank-you process. A follow-up call 30 days later. It's not fluff. It's a reputation-building infrastructure. And the smoother your systems, the more referrals you generate, the more deals come to you pre-warmed, and the more powerful your position becomes in every future conversation. Reputation is a long game, but it pays compounding interest. Your systems are the machine that keeps it growing.

For details on how to systematize your business, go to
https://www.NegotiationDomination.com/Systems

The Unseen Negotiation

So much of what moves the deal forward, what tips the scales in your favor, happens invisibly. Behind the scenes. Before the handshake. After the follow-up. Between the lines.

It's in the tone of your voice. The timing of your emails. The format of your proposal. The language in your contracts. The way your brand shows up consistently across platforms. The trust people have in your name is based on how you handled the last ten deals. The referral from the agent who vouched for your character. The systems that made closing seamless. The thank-you card that made a seller feel respected. None of these things happens at the table. However, they shape what happens because of the table. That's the deeper game, the Maverick game. The one most people never see, and therefore never play.

Final Word: Tilt the Field Before You Step On It

If you think negotiation starts with a phone call and ends with a signature, you're playing checkers while the real players are out here playing chess. The real negotiation isn't about closing hard at the table. It is about tilting the field before you ever step onto it, and keeping that field tilted after you walk away.

So yes—master the scripts, the closes, the psychology. But never forget the terrain you're operating on. If you've laid the groundwork right, positioned your brand, built your relationships, tightened your systems, and stayed consistent across every interaction, then the negotiation doesn't need to be a battle. By the time they sit down with you, the outcome is already in motion. The best deals aren't won at the table. They're won **beyond** it

Each strategy specified in this book can change your negotiations and add thousands to your world… ONLY when it is applied! You want more in your world? You want to create win-win-win deals? You want to win more at the negotiation table? Apply all you have ready and connect with us for more; we are adding every day!

Join us at https://www.NegotiationDomination.com
for more and more negotiation mastery!

BONUS

The Deal Maker's Playbook

10 Maverick Hacks to Win

Negotiation is just the beginning. Once you learn to close a deal, the next level is attracting the right deals before they even happen.

In this bonus chapter, I'll give you the 10 advanced hacks I use to land high-level partnerships, joint ventures, and strategic collaborations with companies, influencers, and rainmakers.

These aren't theories. These are the real-world Maverick moves I've used to secure six- and seven-figure partnerships.

1. The Pre-Frame Power Play

Before the conversation starts, you frame how you want to be seen. Send a one-pager, reel, or bio that positions you as high value. You control the lens before the first handshake.

2. The 3W Rule

Every strategic deal must include a **win** for you, a **win** for them, and a **win** for a third party (like their customers or team). Present this triangle of value in the opening pitch.

3. Maverick Can Opener: ASK WHY

In every pitch meeting, ask: "Why haven't you already done this with someone else?" This surfaces objections early and shows you're thinking like a partner, not a vendor.

4. The Reverse Columbo Close (Oh By the Way)

Instead of asking for a concession, use it to offer something of added value. After the main ask, add a smaller "oh by the way" offer that sounds like an afterthought but is actually a powerful hook. It triggers a "why not" response.

5. The Strategic Seeding

In early conversations, avoid referencing future collaboration: "**When** we do that event together..." or "Once we combine our lists..." It primes their subconscious to believe you're already working together.

6. The 3-Option Offer

Always give three options:

- A premium option that positions you at the top of the game.
- A mid-tier that feels like a win-win.
- A starter option that feels easy to say yes to.+

An adjustment to this technique: suggest three different ways to engage with you: casually, regularly, and intently, locking arms. It demonstrates flexibility and strength.

7. WOW Box
If you really want to close a whale, send a physical box with branded items, a handwritten note, and your offer printed like a contract. It interrupts the digital noise and creates tangible value. WOW them from day one.

8. Lead with Value
Lead with something free that delivers undeniable value. A resource. A contact. A lead. This puts you in the "giver" category and builds fast trust.

9. My TEAM My Family
Make it clear you're not just another deal maker. You have power players behind you who are your family. When you engage with me, you get them as well. They always have my back and, in extension, have yours as well.

10. Power Pause Follow-Up
After your pitch, don't chase. Pause. Let them feel your absence. Then re-engage with a simple, strong follow-up: "Are you ready to make magic happen?"

Use these 10 hacks when you want to level up who you negotiate with, not just what you negotiate for. Dominate the boardroom. Win the stage. Build the empire.

As always, negotiate like a Maverick?

Ready to master this live?
Join me at my next events and step into a room full of deal-makers, investors, coaches, and empire builders. You'll never negotiate the same again. Because once you learn to dominate the deal, you

dominate everything.

https://www.NegotiationDomination.com/Events

About the Author

Paul Finck – The Maverick Millionaire® – is a master known for his mastery of Negotiations, high-stakes influence, a relentless deal-maker, and the go-to strategist for entrepreneurs, real estate investors, and business leaders who want to win big without playing small.

With nearly **40 years in the entrepreneurial arena**, Paul has closed **over $30 million in real estate transactions**, generated **more than $50 million in coaching and informational marketing sales**, and personally hosted **over 250 live bootcamps** and **a thousand+ virtual events** worldwide. He's been featured in **18 best-selling books**, sharing the stage and deal table with some of the biggest names in business, sales, and negotiation.

Paul is the creator of **The Maverick Difference™**, a counter-intuitive, results-driven approach that flips conventional wisdom on its head and produces real-world wins. His client roster spans **real estate moguls, high-end coaches, professionals, top-tier sales teams, and investors**, all of whom turn to Paul when the outcome matters most.

In Negotiation Domination, Paul distills decades of battle-tested experience, behind-closed-doors strategies, and psychological maneuvers into a playbook that works in **any market, any industry, and under any level of pressure**. This is not a theory. This is how Paul has built empires, secured impossible deals, and taught thousands to do the same.

When he's not on stage, running high-level masterminds, or creating multi-million-dollar strategies for his clients, Paul is leading **The Maverick Universe**, an entrepreneur's hub for bold action, accelerated results, and life on your own terms. His mission is simple: **Equip you with the tools, mindset, and maverick edge to win — every time.**

https://www.NegotiationDomination.com

www.ingramcontent.com/pod-product-compliance
Lightning Source LLC
Chambersburg PA
CBHW050656160426
43194CB00010B/1962